Lynn,

friend, neighbor, co-worker,
you add to our lives in
so many ways!
Eph 4:32
Teri Keener Smith

ABOUT THE AUTHOR

Lori Keenen Smith is a retired insurance professional with a heart for creative writing. She has written poems and short stories since childhood. Smith obtained a Journalism degree from the University of Arkansas and currently resides with her husband in Northwest Arkansas after spending many years in Kentucky and Tennessee.

Lorlee's Bee-you-ti-ful Day

By Lori Keenen Smith

Illustrations by Mary K. Routt

Bluebird Press

www.thebluebirdpress.com

Gladewater, Texas

Library of Congress Control Number: 2020917079

ISBN 978-0-9976856-1-9

Cover and interior illustrations by Mary K. Routt

Published by Bluebird Press, LLC
15891 County Road 3110
Gladewater, Texas 75647
www.thebluebirdpress.com

This story is a tribute to people and pets in my life who have made a profound impact. One special kitty, Bazz, will be alive forever, both in my heart and through this story.

A heartfelt thanks to my husband Jerry who shares this journey with me, my father-in-law Bo, my Dad for creating special memories, and to Joe and Ben for their funny stories - all of which have a part in this story. A special thank you to Lauren and Chrissy for their inspiration and encouragment.

Lorlee was enjoying the day flying through the big blue sky. She twirled and dipped and let out a big sigh of contentment.

"What a BEE-YOU-TI-FUL day!!!"

The warm sunshine bathed the flowers and trees in sunlight and the birds were singing sweet songs.

The only thing that could make this day any better would be to finally find a place to call home.

Out of nowhere Lorlee crashed into something BIG, BROWN, SNORTING, and BREATHING SMOKE!

As she back-pedaled in the air to figure out what had happened, a strange beast eyed her grimly and growled in a deep voice,

"I DON'T
like
bees!"

Smoke came out of his nose with every HUFF as he remembered the time he swatted a bee with his tail and it flew right back and STUNG him!
"I DON'T like bees!" he declared again.

"I'm very sorry, sir," Lorlee said. "I didn't mean you any harm."

"Well, watch where you are going next time... **AND DON'T BOTHER ME AGAIN!**" the beast said gruffly as he turned to walk away.

Lorlee gathered her composure and started to fly away when she saw her friend Bazz in the distance resting under a weeping cherry tree. She had not seen Bazz in such a long time.

"**Bazz!**" she yelled out as she flew toward him in excitment.

Bazz, awakened by the voice, yawned and stretched before he looked up to notice Lorlee flying toward him.

When he saw her, he jumped to his feet and joyfully bounded through the grass to meet her.

"**LORLEE!** What are you doing here? I've missed you so much! It's been SUCH a long time."

Lorlee told him about all she had seen as she flew, dipped, twirled, and enjoyed the nice day. But then she told Bazz about the scary beast who growled and blew smoke out of his nose.

Bazz was startled at the thought of such a beast and asked Lorlee to show him **EXACTLY** where she saw it. He certainly did **NOT** want to make the same mistake and accidentally run into such an

AWFUL,
       FRIGHTENING
              beast,
                  too!

Lorlee flew close to Bazz for protection, and Bazz walked timidly next to Lorlee. They were definitely heading in the right direction to where Lorlee had crashed into the beast...

...but when they topped the hill, they did not see him. They both sighed in relief and began to laugh, play, and talk.

"Where do you live now?"
Lorlee asked.

"A kind couple adopted me and gave me a real home. They give me a soft bed every night, lots of food, and more love than I've ever known before. What makes me the happiest is when they hold me, cuddle me and talk to me," Bazz responded.

Lorlee longed for the kind of love he was describing. She never had any real friends besides Bazz. Everyone always seemed to shoo her away because bees were known to sting.

After pausing to ponder this, she said, "I wonder if they would let **ME** stay? This sounds like such a great place to live...well...except for that beast."

Lorlee suddenly buzzed in fright!

"THE BEAST!!!"

Bazz turned to look, but he only saw Max, the bull that lived there. Bazz was puzzled and asked, "Is **THIS** the beast you were talking about??"

"YES! And he certainly doesn't like bees! *RUUUUN!!!*" Lorlee exclaimed frantically.

Bazz smiled and laughed as he explained, "Max is only a bull. He's grumpy and can act mean but he's really not that bad...

...You see, bulls have to act tough because they help protect the babies in their herd. He may be different than you and me, but he has an important role that only **HE** can do."

"Hey Max!" Bazz yelled. "Good to see you today!" They walked toward each other and Bazz sat down boldly in front of him without any fear at all.

The big bull leaned down and gently touched noses with him. Bazz purred and Max lit up with a smile.

Max liked Bazz a lot and let him walk in and out of his legs without stepping on him or hurting him.

Bazz told Max that Lorlee was a very good friend of his and introduced them to one another. Max grumbled and growled, "I **DON'T** like bees. But I will try to be nice since she is your friend."

Bazz rubbed against Max's leg and purred. "Thank you, Max. She is very important even though she is small. The world needs bees like Lorlee, you know?"

"Why is that?" Max snorted. "Bees are so small and insignificant! All they're good for, as far as I know, is stinging me on the rump!"

Bazz laughed and said, "Well, without bees, you wouldn't have all of these beautiful flowers and plants to eat for one!

Bees take pollen from plant to plant allowing them to reproduce and thrive. That means they help produce fruits, vegetables, nuts, seeds, and so much more!"

Bazz continued, "That's not even considering the fact that they use some of that pollen to make honey which tastes **SOOOO** sweet!"

"Bees are very important for the well-being of many things we love and enjoy."

Lorlee flew up to Max's head and landed on one of his horns. She buzzed and giggled and told Max she would be kind to him.

"You know, Max, we bees only sting if we think someone is trying to hurt us, just like you only charge toward someone with your horns if you think they are trying to hurt you or the herd. If we feel safe and loved, we will naturally love right back! We need love just like everyone else."

Max softened, "I guess it wasn't right for me to judge all bees from one action. You're so much more than a stinging bee, just like I am so much more than an angry, charging bull. You have a great purpose and a big heart, even though you're small."

Lorlee melted, "Aw, Max! You might be a big, tough bull, but you sure have surprised me by having a kind, soft heart. I think now that we are seeing the good in each other and the benefit of our differences, we are going to be great friends!"

Bazz interjected, "Speaking of love, Lorlee, come with me and I'll show you the kind couple that adopted me and I'll ask if they will adopt YOU, too!"

So after saying goodbye to Max, off they went.

When they found the couple, Lorlee noticed the man's name was printed on his clothes.

"Is his name 'Big Smith'?" she asked Bazz.

"Yes it is!" Bazz said. "How did you know?"

Lorlee explained that she read his name on his clothes.
She loved to read and then spell all the words!

Suddenly, Lorlee and Bazz were tossed in the air unexpectedly as something **BIG** ⟩⟩ ran into them!

Bazz landed perfectly on all four paws just as ⟨⟨ cats are known to do, and Lorlee twisted and turned in the air until she was right side up again.

Bazz sighed and shook his head and then laughed as he licked his fur back into place.

"Don't worry, that's just Coach. He's Big Smith's dog and best friend."

"Is...is...is he friendly?" Lorlee stammered.

"He is very friendly!" Bazz said. "But he's different than us. Coach is quite clumsy! He runs and jumps without looking where he is going and drools on me sometimes too! But he's always happy, accepting of everyone, and a big ball of fun!

"He may be a wrecking ball sometimes, but he sure can put a smile on my face! He's important, too, because he brings such joy and is a friend of everyone around here."

The commotion got the attention of Big Smith and his wife, Lady Smith. Bazz went to them and after some petting and purring, asked if Lorlee could stay.

They responded, "Of course Lorlee can stay! We would love to have her here. We have lots of flowers, trees, and crops that need her help. If she has more family, they are certainly welcome here, too."

Lorlee was SO excited!

Big Smith and Lady Smith had officially invited her to stay! She planned to tell her family immediately and have them come. "They're going to love it here!" she thought. "I can't wait to introduce them to Bazz, Coach, Big Smith, Lady Smith, and yes, even Max!"

Her bee family would finally have a place where they would be loved and accepted for who they are.

Lorlee and Bazz dreamed in excitement of the life they would soon have together. Even though they were so very different, they would always be best friends and watch out for one another.

Lorlee felt a fresh happiness as she flew, twirled, dipped, giggled, and buzzed in the warm sunshine knowing she finally had a real home where she would be very loved.

Lorlee, Bazz, and Max all learned
an important lesson on this
BEE-YOU-TI-FUL day:

No matter how
SMALL,
BIG,
or **DIFFERENT**
someone is,

we all have a very important
purpose in this world...

even if we can't always see it.

THE END